BRAIN GAMES® kids

Amazing Activity Book

Phoenix International Publications, Inc.

Chicago • London • New York • Hamburg • Mexico City • Paris • Sydney

Illustrations: Robin Boyer, Karen Stormer Brooks, Peter Brosshauser, Mattia Cerato, Garry Colby, Mike Dammer, Dave Garbot, Dani Jones, Larry Jones, Kevin Kelly, Robbie Short, Jamie Smith, Chuck Whelon, K Kreto/Shutterstock.com (pattern on cover)

Phoenix International Publications, Inc.
8501 West Higgins Road   59 Gloucester Place
Chicago, Illinois 60631   London W1U 8JJ

www.pikidsmedia.com

p i kids is a trademark of Phoenix International Publications, Inc., and is registered in the United States.

ISBN: 978-1-5037-4926-9

Manufactured in China.

8 7 6 5 4 3 2 1

LET THE PUZZLE FUN BEGIN!

Do you enjoy finding your way through a twisting and turning maze?

How about creating fun and wacky doodles?

And what about connecting numbered dots to reveal cool scenes?

• With *Brain Games® Kids: Amazing Activity Book*, you can do all that—and more!

Every page of this book is like a brand-new adventure. One minute you're leading the alien Zoob through the cosmos in a zigzagging maze, the next you're searching for super hero words and unscrambling codes. Sometimes there are multiple puzzles on a page, and sometimes there is just one large puzzle to tackle. No need to worry if you happen to get stuck; just turn to the back of the book and find the answer you need there.

Are you ready?
Turn the page and dive into your first puzzle adventure—the first of many!

WILD AND WACKY Waterslide

Ride the slide with the bears from top to bottom. When you come to a letter, write it in the boxes below!

Start →

Answers on page 34.

Answers on page 34.

5

NEED FOR SPEED

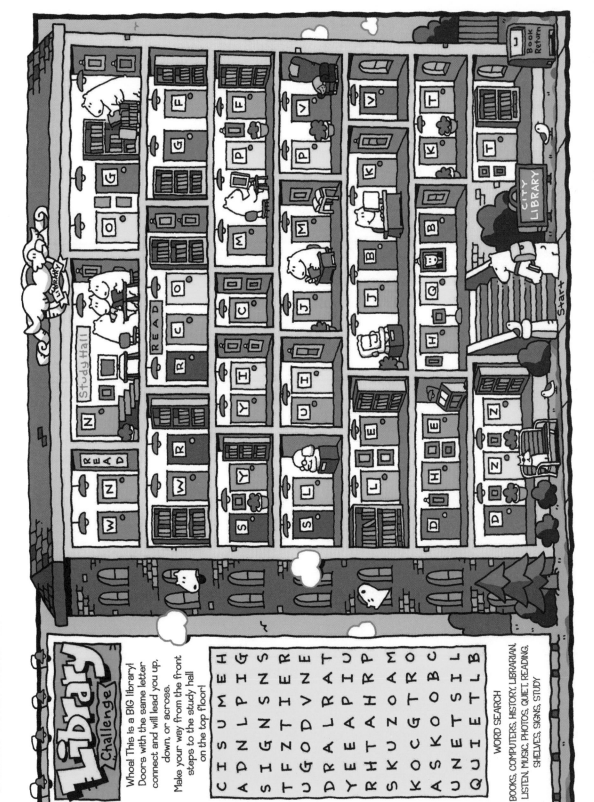

Library Challenge

Whoa! This is a BIG library! Doors with the same letter connect and will lead you up, down, or across.

Make your way from the front steps to the study hall on the top floor!

WORD SEARCH

```
C I S U M E H
A D N L P I G
S I G N S N S
T F Z T I E R
U G O D V N E
D R A L R A T
Y E E A P I U
R H T A H R P
S K U Z O A M
K O C G T R O
A S K O O B C
U N E T S I L
Q U I E T L B
```

BOOKS, COMPUTERS, HISTORY, LIBRARIAN, LISTEN, MUSIC, PHOTOS, QUIET, READING, SHELVES, SIGNS, STUDY

Answers on page 34.

SPACED OUT

Answers on page 35.

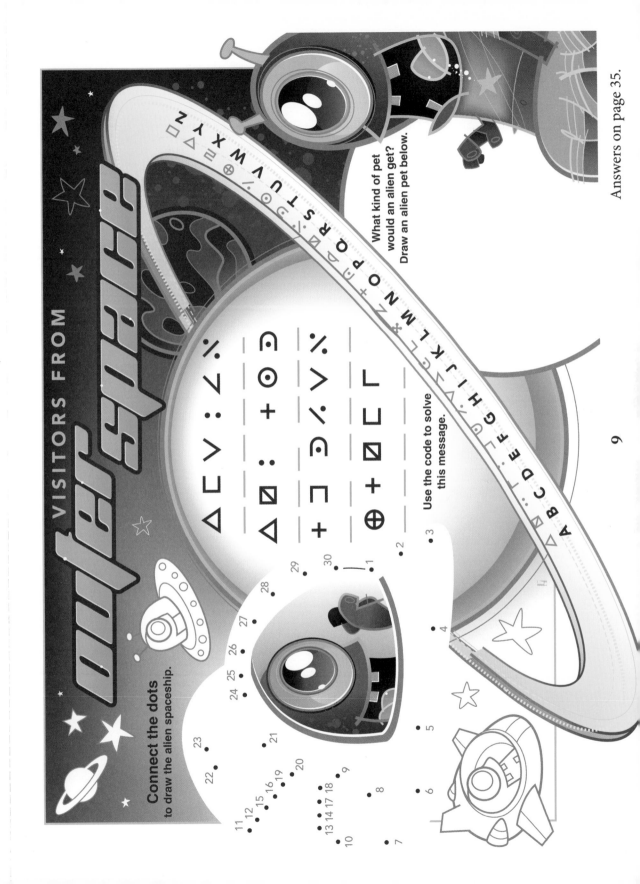

VISITORS FROM outer space

Connect the dots
to draw the alien spaceship.

Use the code to solve
this message.

What kind of pet
would an alien get?
Draw an alien pet below.

A B C D E F G H I J K L M N O P Q R S T U V W X Y Z

Answers on page 35.

9

LINK THE DOTS
Find the hidden figure.

ALL THE WAY UP IN THE SKY
Look at the skyscrapers.
Which is the tallest?
Which is the shortest?

Of all these houses, only two are exactly alike. Can you find them?

BRIDGE MAZE
Make your way over the bridge to get to the other side.

START

FINISH

A DAY IN THE CITY

BRIDGE
CITY

Where's the driver going, toward the city or the bridge? Have fun coloring him as you like!

Answers on page 35.

Tookie Bird Safari

Help the explorers find the sneaky Tookie Bird.

START

FINISH

Answers on page 35.

11

Back to the Hive!

This honeybee is lost in the garden. Help him find his way back to the hive by tracing the correct blue line.

Start

What's the Message?

Use the code to fill in the letters on the lines below to reveal a message just for you!

A E F H L O
P R S T W

Answers on page 36.

Butterfly Flutter

Finish the rest of this butterfly, using the first half as a guide.

LET'S MAKE A PIZZA!

Answers on page 36.

14

The Wild West

Which of these two rootin'-tootin' cowpokes roped the moon? Who roped the sun?

Which hat appears the most along this border?

15

Go for the Goal!

Answers on page 36.

OH MUMMY!

This mummy went on a trip, but he can't remember how to get home! Help him find his way, but first stop at the grocery store and then at the vet to pick up his pooch.

VET!

Start

Finish

Grocery!

FIND THE TWO CAMELS THAT MATCH!

1. 2. 3. 4. 5. 6. 7. 8. 9. 10.

Answers on page 37.

ALIEN INTELLIGENCE

Answers on page 37.

18

IN THE AGE OF DINOSAURS

THERE ARE 10 DINOSAUR EGGS SCATTERED THROUGHOUT THIS PICTURE. CAN YOU FIND THEM?

CAN YOU FIND THE 10 DIFFERENCES BETWEEN THESE 2 PICTURES?

CONNECT THE DOTS TO SEE WHAT'S COMING OUT OF THE EGG!

Answers on page 37.

up in the sky!

Color the scene below!

Help Superdude follow the maze to return the eggs to their nest.

Follow the strings to match a Kite with each Kid!

1

2

3

A

B

C

Answers on page 38.

FE-FI-FO-FUM!

Help this poor giant get his goose back from that **THIEVIN' JACK!**

START
(Don't cross any yellow lines!)

FINISH!

Unscramble these Fairy-Tale Folks!

INREDLACEL _____

ETH HETER TILELT SIGP _____

LIPEGESN TAYEBU _____

TREEP NAP _____

IHOPCOINC _____

NWSO THEWI _____

HEMROT OSOGE _____

VTMUPH PUDTYM _____

EHT IGB DBA FOWL _____

Answers on page 38.

23

FINISH !!!

SNAIL RACE

Snails are known for being slow, but this time they are racing against each other! Write their position in the race in the boxes on the left.

CAUGHT IN THE WEB

It's not too late for this little fly! Help her find her way through the spider's web to break free.

START

CREEPY CRAWLIES

FLOWER PATH

This butterfly wants to reach the flower. There are three possible paths, but only one takes her there. Which one?

a b

c

SHOES, SHOES, SHOES!

Wow! This caterpillar needs shoes. How many will he need to buy? Count his feet and circle the right answer, then have fun coloring!

38   40   44

Answers on page 38.

Answers on page 39.

25

Answers on page 39.

26

Answers on page 39.

27

A TRIP TO THE ZOO

YIKES! THE ANIMALS HAVE TAKEN LETTERS FROM SIGNS AROUND THE ZOO! PLEASE MATCH THE LETTER TO EACH ANIMAL IN THE BLANKS TO ANSWER THIS QUESTION: **WHAT DO DOLPHINS WEAR TO KEEP WARM?**

CHANGE ONE LETTER PER WORD TO TRANSFORM THIS SWEET LITTLE DEER INTO A FEROCIOUS LION!!

DEER

_ _ _ _ TERM OF AFFECTION

_ _ _ _ SHAKESPEARE KING

_ _ _ _ TO REST ON

_ _ _ _ TO LEND MONEY

_ _ _ _ LARGE WATERBIRD

LION

CAN YOU FIND THE ONE CAMEL THAT MATCHES THIS SHADOW EXACTLY?

Answers on page 39.

COMIC BOOK HEROES

Unscramble the letters to discover what many comic book heroes have.

CESTER NITTYEDI

_ _ _ _ _ _ _ _ _ _ _ _

Help this hero find his way through this maze to catch the bandit.

START

Find the five hidden masks on this page.

Find the eight things a comic book hero might have.

G	A	D	G	E	T	S	H
C	R	T	L	S	S	R	P
A	C	A	I	W	O	C	O
B	H	A	B	G	I	O	W
L	E	R	P	O	H	S	E
O	N	C	A	E	L	T	R
G	E	M	X	A	D	U	S
O	M	A	S	K	R	M	A
C	Y	A	O	T	R	E	J

ARCHENEMY
CAPE
COSTUME
GADGETS
LOGO
MASK
POWERS
TIGHTS

Answers on page 40.

29

Pirates!!

There are 10 bones hidden in the picture. Find them or walk the plank!

Aaargh Matey! Copy the pictures in each numbered square into the same numbered square in the grid.

There are 20 things in this picture that start with a "p." Can you find them?

Answers on page 40.

30

Pirate Puzzle

Answers on page 40.

31

MECHANICAL DRAWINGS

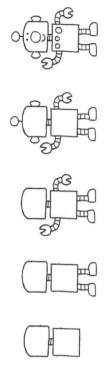

Draw this robot in six easy steps. Make lots of robots, or draw a futuristic scene around your mechanical friend for even more doodle fun.

33

ANSWERS

Need for Speed (page 6)

Wild and Wacky Waterslide (page 4)

Library Challenge (page 7)

Abracadabra (page 5)

Spaced Out (page 8)

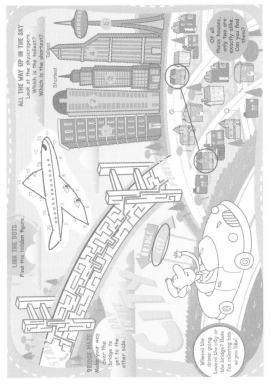

A Day in the City (page 10)

Visitors from Outer Space (page 9)

Tookie Bird Safari (page 11)

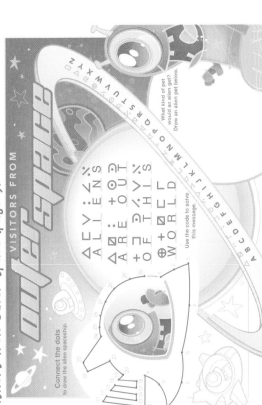

35

The Wild West (page 15)

What's the Message? (page 12)

Go for the Goal! (page 16)

Let's Make a Pizza! (page 14)

Oh Mummy! (page 17)

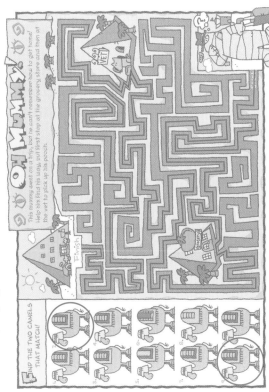

Big Top Challenge! (page 19)

Alien Intelligence (page 18)

In the Age of Dinosaurs (page 20)

37

Fe-Fi-To-Fum! (page 23)

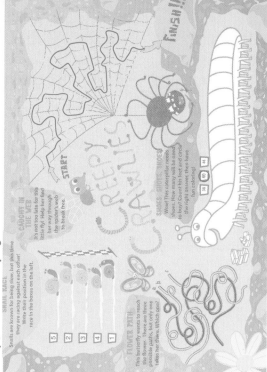

Help this poor giant get his goose back from that **Thievin' Jack!**

START (Don't use any yellow lines!)

FINISH!

Unscramble these Fairy-Tale Folks!

NIREDLACEL	Cinderella
ETH HEETER TILELT SGIP	The Three Little Pigs
LIPGEGSN TAYEBU	Sleeping Beauty
TRREP NAP	Peter Pan
HOISCOMIC	Pinocchio
NWSO THEWI	Snow White
HEOMRDT OSRODE	Mother Goose
YTMUPH PUDDTYM	Humpty Dumpty
EHT IGB DBA FOWL	The Big Bad Wolf

Up in the Sky! (page 21)

Follow the string to match a kite with each kid!

Help Superdude follow the maze to return the egg to their nest!

up in the sky!

Creepy Crawlies (page 24)

CREEPY CRAWLIES

FINISH!!

START

CAUGHT IN THE WEB
It's not too late for this little fly! Help her find her way through the spider's web to break free.

SNAIL RACE.
Snails are known for being slow, but this time they are racing against each other! Write their position in the race in the boxes on the left.

5 2 3 4 1

FLOWER PATH
This butterfly wants to reach the flower. There are three possible paths, but only one takes her there. Which one?

SHOE, SHOE, SHOES!
Wow! This caterpillar needs shoes. How many will he need to buy? Count his feet and circle the right answer, then have fun coloring!

Time to Dine! (page 22)

Time to Dine!

38

Quest for Fuel (page 25)

Fun at the Beach (page 26)

Tree House Maze-o-Rama (page 27)

A Trip to the Zoo (page 28)

Pirate Puzzle (page 31)

The Great Dino Cookie Chase (page 32)

Comic Book Heroes (page 29)

Pirates!! (page 30)